The Complete Encyclopedia Of Socialist Wisdom

Dr. Robert Owens

Cover Design

Dr. Robert Owens

Dedication

This book is dedicated to all the millions of
Americans who work hard every day to
make America great again, and to those
patriots who have not lost hope.

Acknowledgement

I want to acknowledge the only economy
that really matters: the economy of God
and that any of us who think we're movers
and shakers need to realize that History is
really His Story from beginning to end.

The Complete Encyclopedia
Of Socialist Wisdom

1

The wisdom of Socialism alphabetically arranged for easy access and ready reference:

A:

The Complete Encyclopedia
Of Socialist Wisdom

2

B:

C:

The Complete Encyclopedia
Of Socialist Wisdom

D:

5

E:

F:

7

G:

H:

I:

The Complete Encyclopedia
Of Socialist Wisdom

10

J:

11

K:

The Complete Encyclopedia
Of Socialist Wisdom

12

L:

M:

14

N:

The Complete Encyclopedia
Of Socialist Wisdom

15

O:

P:

17

Q:

R:

S:

T:

U:

22

V:

23

W:

X:

Y:

26

Z:

Suggested Reading

The following exhaustive list contains the names of the selfless exponents of central planning, statism, and the forced redistribution of wealth that are worth reading. They have labored throughout History for power over their fellow man, strangling regulations, and the stifling bureaucracy needed to build their own kingdoms on foundations of sand. The works of these philosophers, economists, authors, and savants are must reading for anyone seeking the deep and abiding wisdom Socialism.

The Complete Encyclopedia
Of Socialist Wisdom

The Complete Encyclopedia
Of Socialist Wisdom

The Complete Encyclopedia
Of Socialist Wisdom

The Complete Encyclopedia
Of Socialist Wisdom

31

32

The Complete Encyclopedia
Of Socialist Wisdom

33

34

The Complete Encyclopedia
Of Socialist Wisdom

The Complete Encyclopedia
Of Socialist Wisdom

The Complete Encyclopedia
Of Socialist Wisdom

The Complete Encyclopedia
Of Socialist Wisdom

38

The Complete Encyclopedia
Of Socialist Wisdom

Conclusion

In the long and dismal History of human bondage an unbroken chain of command economies and tyrants kept their boot on the neck of humanity.

Then came the American experiment, the spirit of 76, the miracle at Philadelphia, and for brief moment in the hours of human bondage the flame of freedom flickered and then blazed, lighting the way to a new age: the Age of Liberty. Unfettered by central planning and tyranny the ingenuity and enterprise of man brought forth in two short centuries more innovation and accomplishment than the previous eons of slavery.

Then the American Socialist who call themselves Progressives, who want the power to dictate the lives of others for goals they say are for the betterment of others but which in reality are merely tools they use to gain power began to systematically re-forge the shackles.

Through manipulation of the media and control of education the Progressives gained the tacit approval of the general population. Most people were too busy working and living their lives to keep their attention on the wider society. The prosperity freedom created bred generations of people who began to take it for granted. Today after cycles of neglect incubated through years of sports-addicted couch potatoes clamoring for ever greater doses of bread and circuses we have a mass of citizens who follow like sheep to the slaughter or lemmings to the cliff anywhere the Progressive puppet masters portray as the next free entitlement.

Written to establish and maintain a limited government with our heads in the sand we pretend that the Constitution is still in force. In reality we have imperial presidents ruling by decree, a Congress that abdicated all its power to either the President or the bureaucracy, a judiciary that assumed the power to overturn laws and re-write the Constitution through interpretation any time they want. We live in a dysfunctional oligarchy masquerading as a functional republic. We flounder and lurch from one crisis to the next on the world stage because we're divorced from our principles and hypnotized into believing we still stand for freedom when we're a front for multi-national corporations and international banks. A giant hobbled by pygmies unable to understand that by discarding our heritage of personal liberty, individual freedom, and economic opportunity we've made ourselves no different from every other plunder empire that's fallen from Rome to Britain.

We've descended into mediocrity by adopting the same over regulated, "From everyone according to their ability to everyone according to their need" pathology that doomed the commissars with their five-year plans, gulags, and iron curtains. Whenever this rob from the rich to give to the poor looting of producers to support non-producers runs into trouble, which is whenever they run out of other people's money, they blame

Capitalism, the goose that lays the golden eggs. In a classic bait and switch the Progressive collectivists offer freedom and deliver regulations. They offer prosperity and deliver stagnation, inflation, and economic ruin. Our rob Peter to pay Paul pied pipers blame Capitalism when in reality Socialism is the problem and Capitalism is the solution.

This progressive slide into the dustbin of History will only be reversed by applying the opposing force of freedom. This must include the freedom of action, freedom of association, of speech, thought, and the freedom to excel.

If we outlaw failure with a security net of social programs we ensure that some will turn it into a hammock. When borders dissolve and we drown in an avalanche should we really watch in disbelief as the programs our elected masters have implemented turn the greatest nation the world has ever known into a third world hellhole saluting the stars and stripes and repeating like a robot, "We're number one!"

Enjoy these other books by Dr. Owens

Political Commentary:

The Constitution Failed

Constitutional Philosophy in Action

Then Came Trump

Drain the Swamp

History:

America Won the Vietnam War

The Azusa Street Revival

The More Things Change The More They Stay The Same

America: Vol 1 Colonial American History

COGIC History: The Dark Years

Religion:

Faith

Novels:

1.   America's Trojan War (Series

2.   America's Odyssey: You Can't Go Home Again

3.   America's Odyssey II: You Must Go Home Again

4.   America's Steel Horse Brigade

5.   America's Armageddon

All these titles are available from Amazon in paperback and Kindle